Teacher's Resource Book

Level Pre-K

Blackline Masters

A Division of The McGraw-Hill Companies

Columbus, Ohio

www.sra4kids.com

SRA/McGraw-Hill

A Division of The McGraw-Hill Companies

Send all inquiries to:
SRA/McGraw-Hill
8787 Orion Place
Columbus, OH 43240-4027

Printed in the United States of America.

0-07-584254-8

1 2 3 4 5 6 7 8 9 MAL 09 08 07 06 05 04 03

Table of Contents

Unit 1 — I'm Special!

Unit 2 — Families Everywhere

Unit 3 — All Kinds of Friends

Unit 4 — Helping Hands

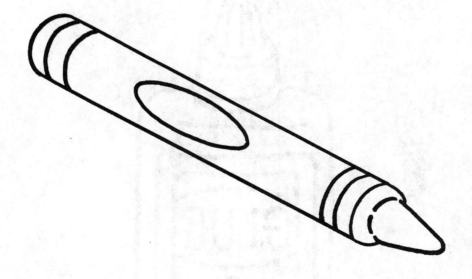

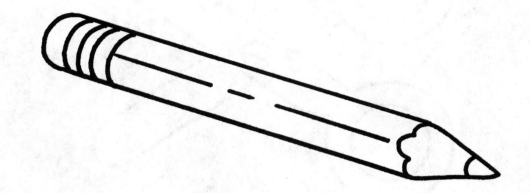

GLUE

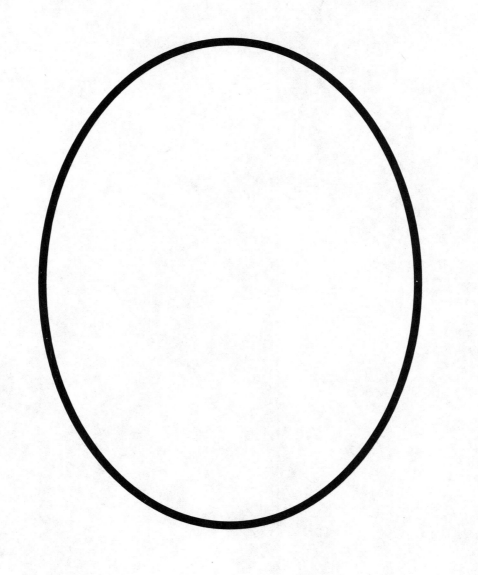

My name is _____.

Here are _____'s hands.

My favorite food is _____.

I Am Special

_____

I am happy.

Name _____

UNIT I

I'm Special!

Name_____

I like to wear _____.

Name

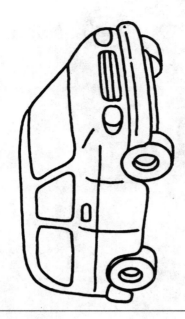

I like to go to _____.

All About Me

Written and Drawn by

_____

13

Name

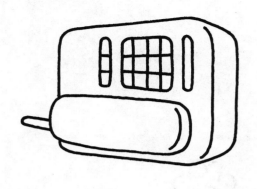

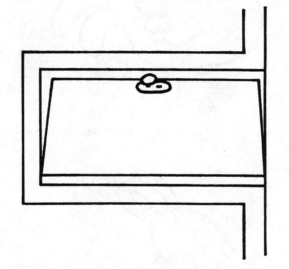

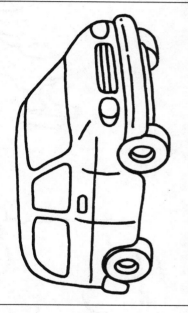

UNIT I   **I'm Special!**

Name_____

Name_____

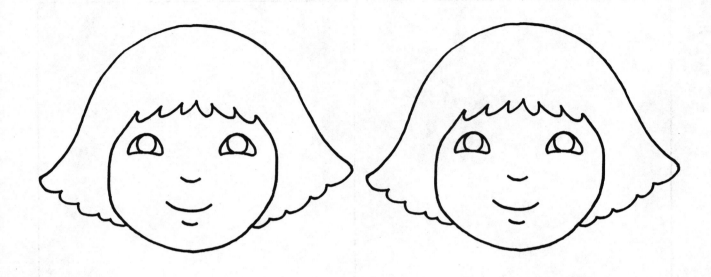

I have fun by myself.

I take care of myself.

Name_____

I like my _____.

I Like Myself

Written and Drawn by

_____

My Family

Drawn by _____

I like to _____
with my family.

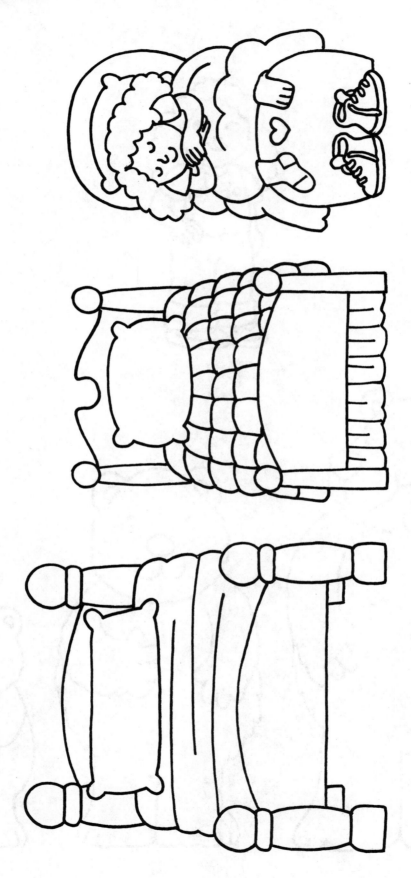

Come to Our Celebration of Families

To: _____

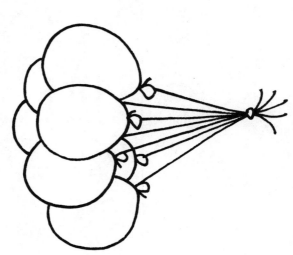

Date: _____

Time: _____

Place: _____

From: _____

I Love You,

_____

I share my _____
with my friends.

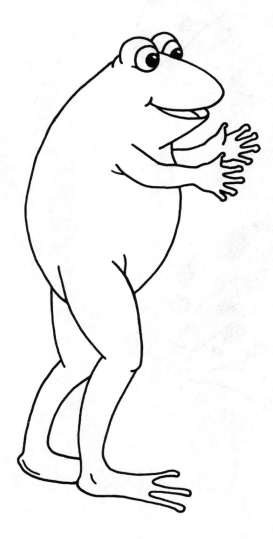
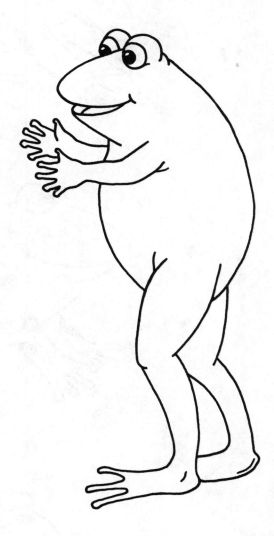

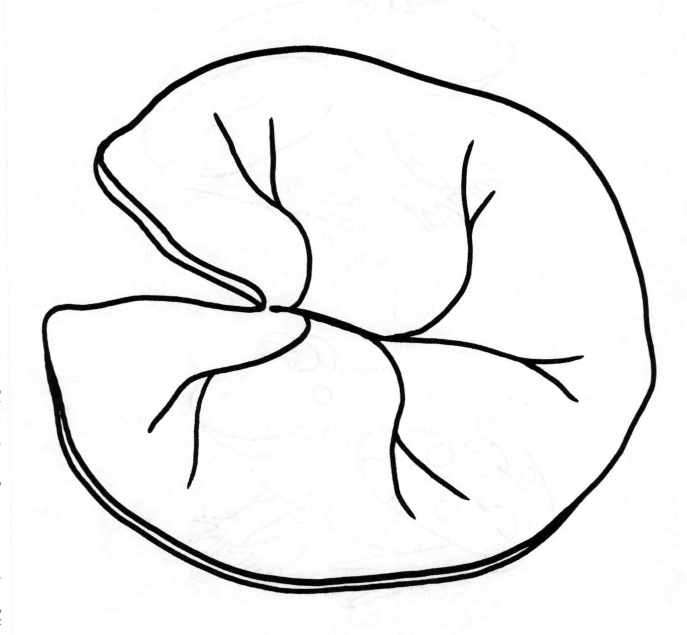

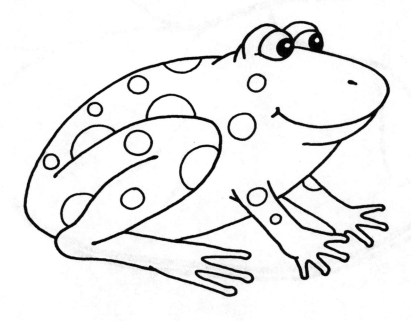

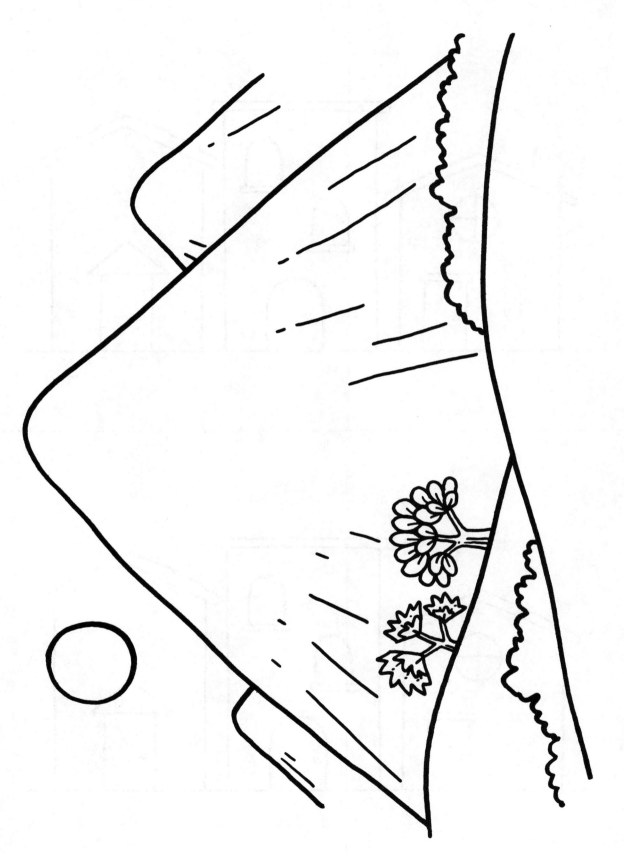

39

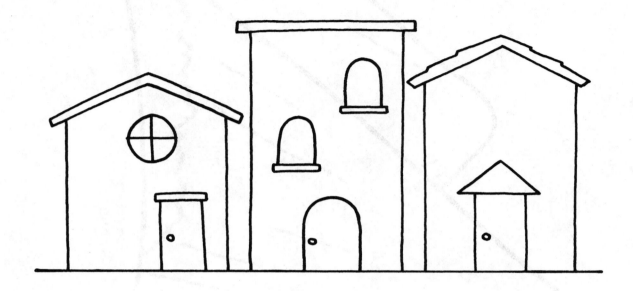

My bear is brown.

My rabbit is yellow.

Name_____

My crocodile is green.

My Kangaroo Is Blue

Written and Drawn by

_____

UNIT 4 **Helping Hands**

UNIT 4   Helping Hands

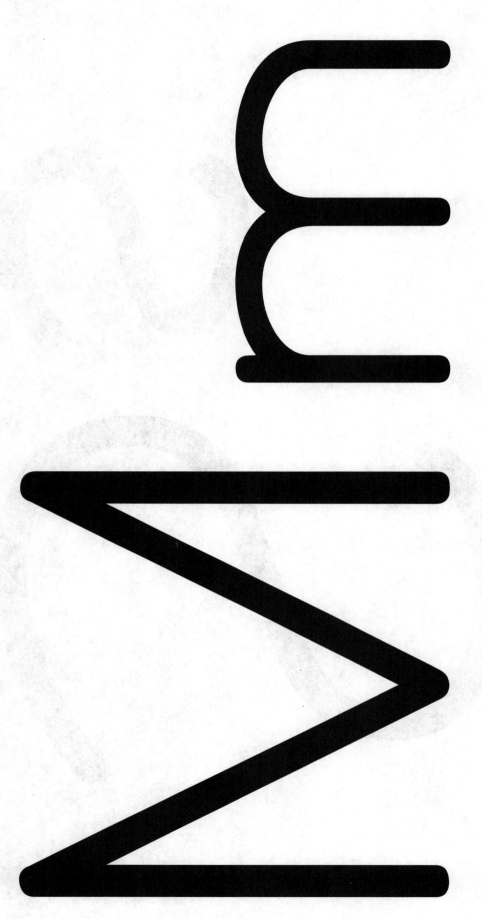

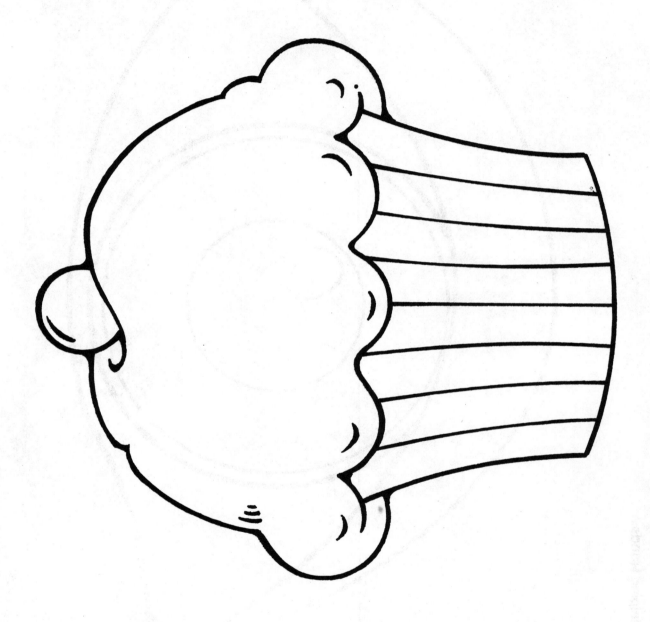

Teacher's Resource Book

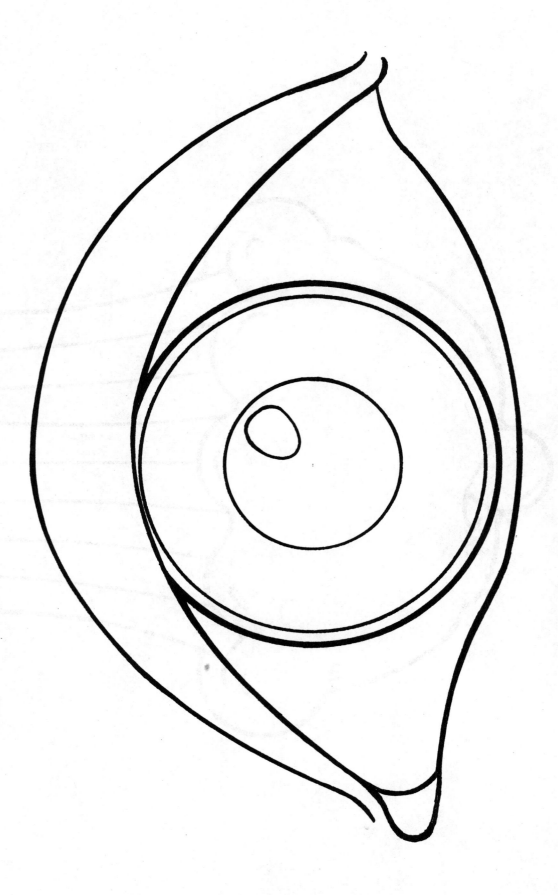

UNIT 4   Helping Hands

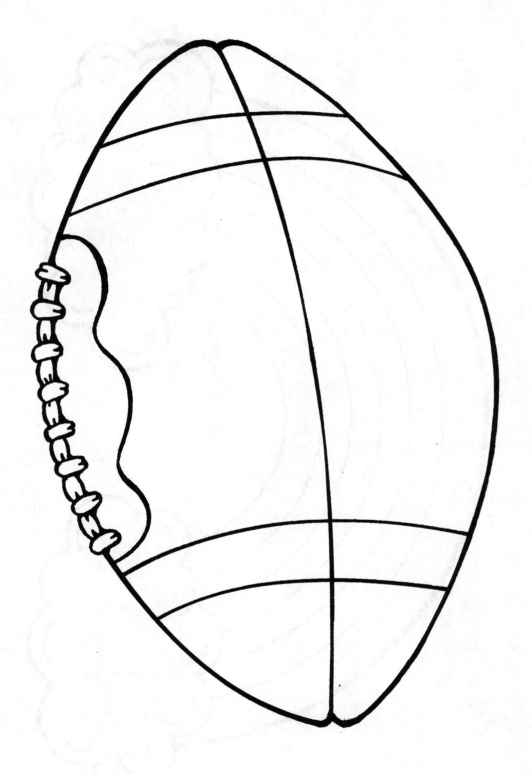

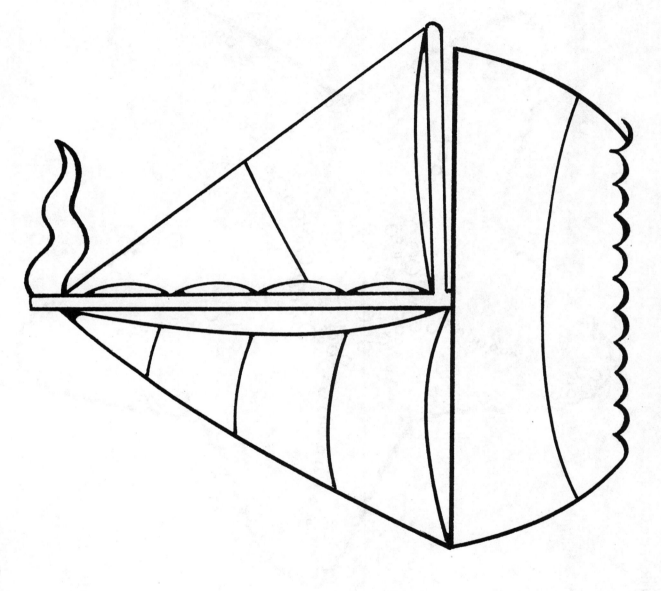

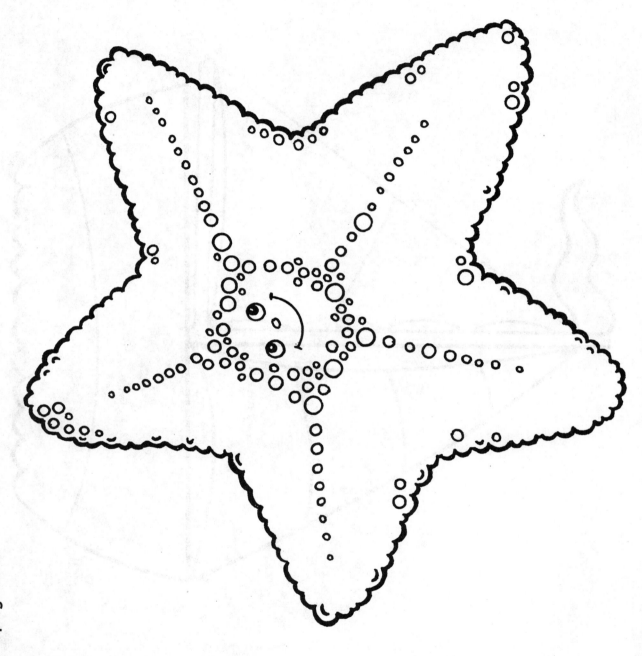

Teacher's Resource Book

UNIT 4 Helping Hands

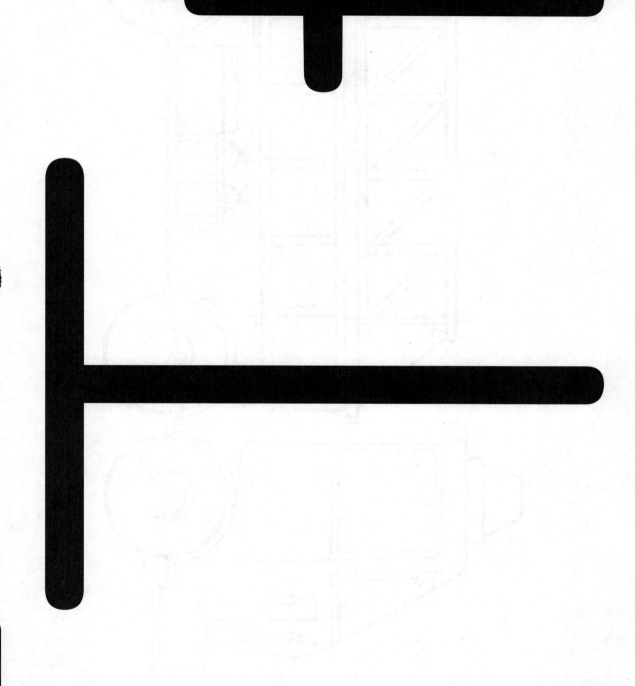

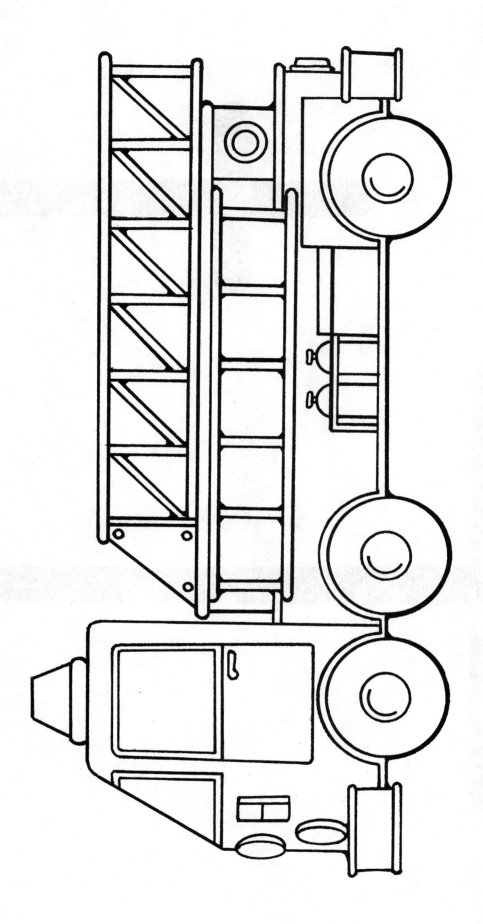

Name

Name_____

Dot has _____spots.

UNIT 4 Helping Hands

Helping Hands

_____'s Helping Hands

I take a taxi to _____ .

UNIT 5

Let's Go!

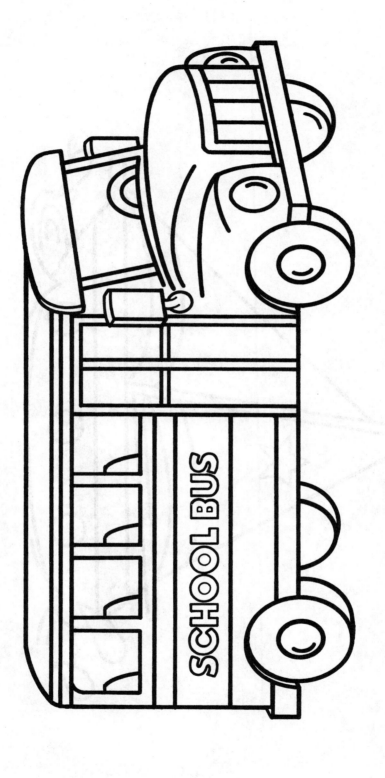

The school bus

UNIT 5   Let's Go!

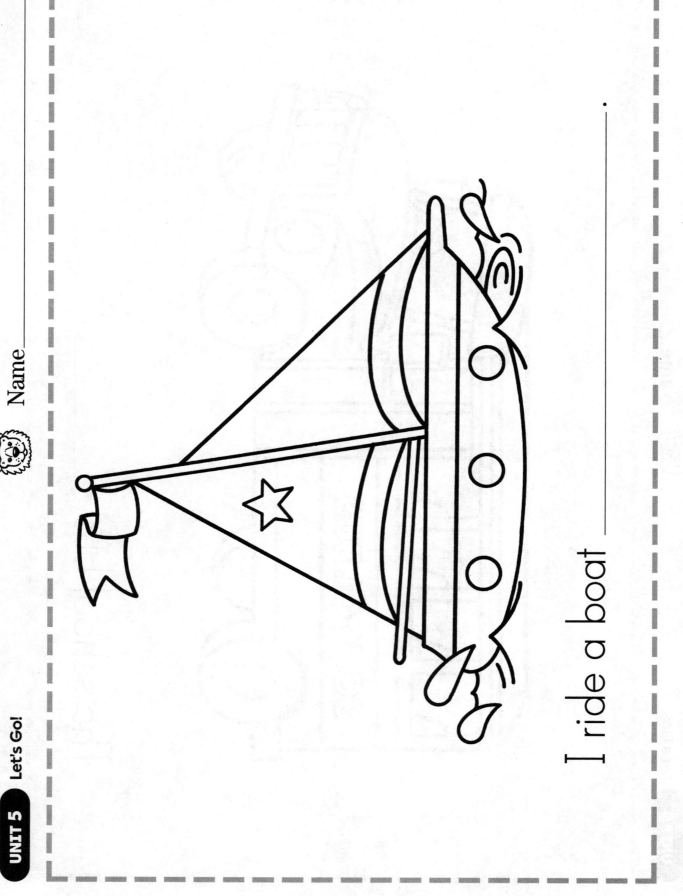

I ride a boat _____.

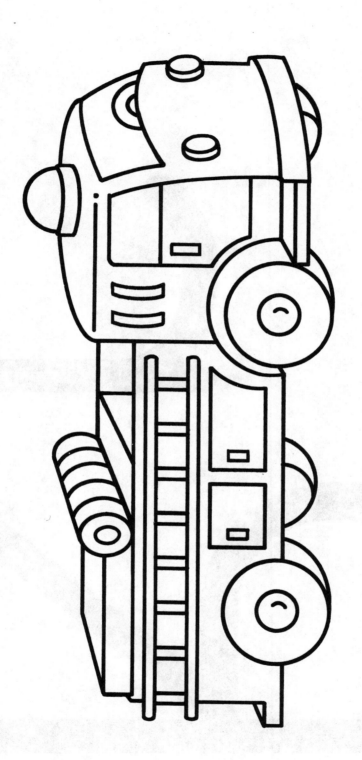

A fire engine

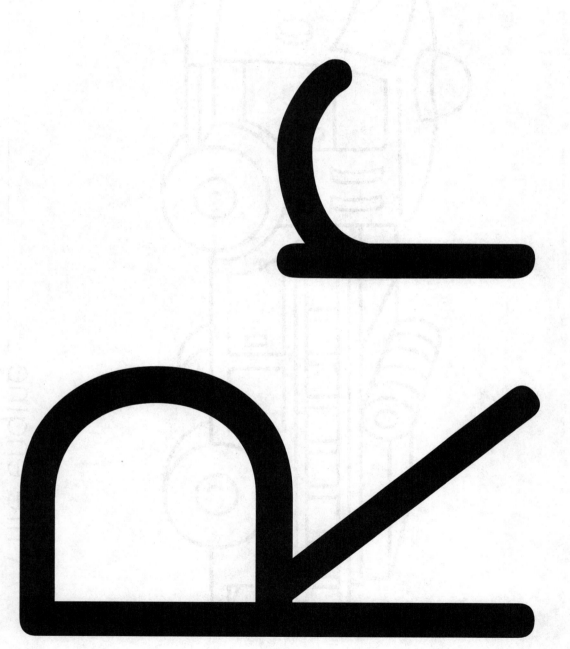

UNIT 5

Let's Go!

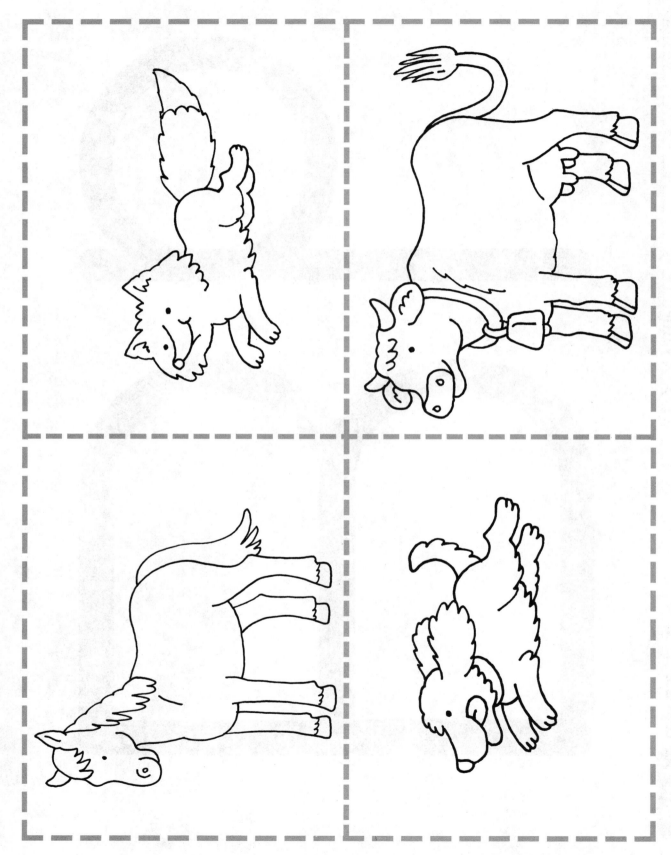

71

72

UNIT 5 · Let's Go!

73

Name_____

I can go _____ on a bike.

I can ride skates _____.

Name_____

I carry _____ in a wagon.

I ride _____ on a scooter.

UNIT 5 Let's Go!

UNIT 5

Let's Go!

I'm on the go!

Name_____

See

Smell

Taste

Hear

Touch

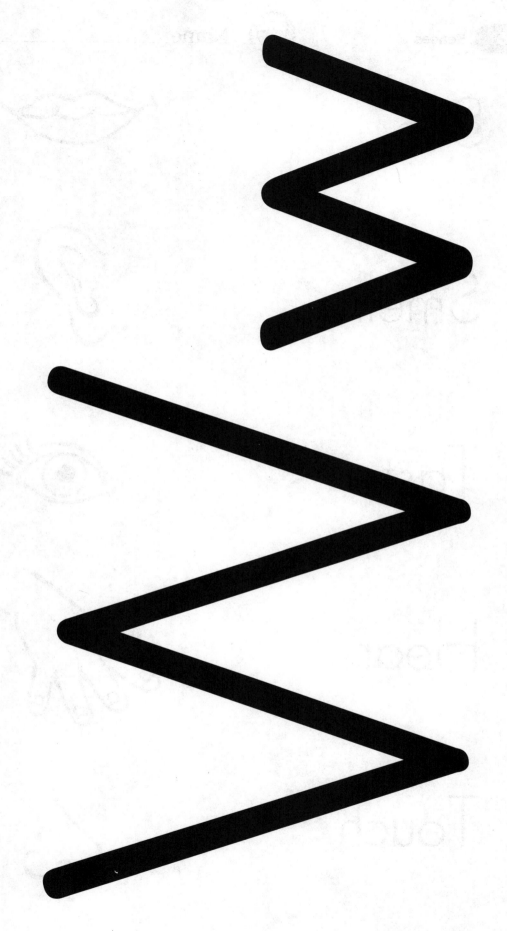

UNIT 6 Senses

Teacher's Resource Book

My Senses

Written and Drawn by

_____

UNIT 6 Senses

Name _____

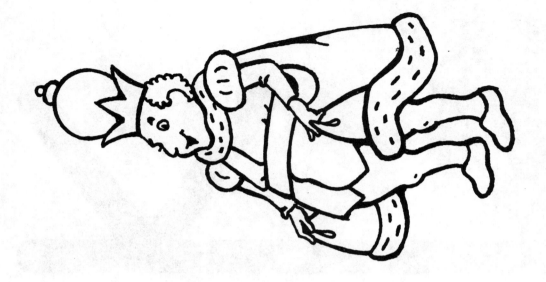

87

Name

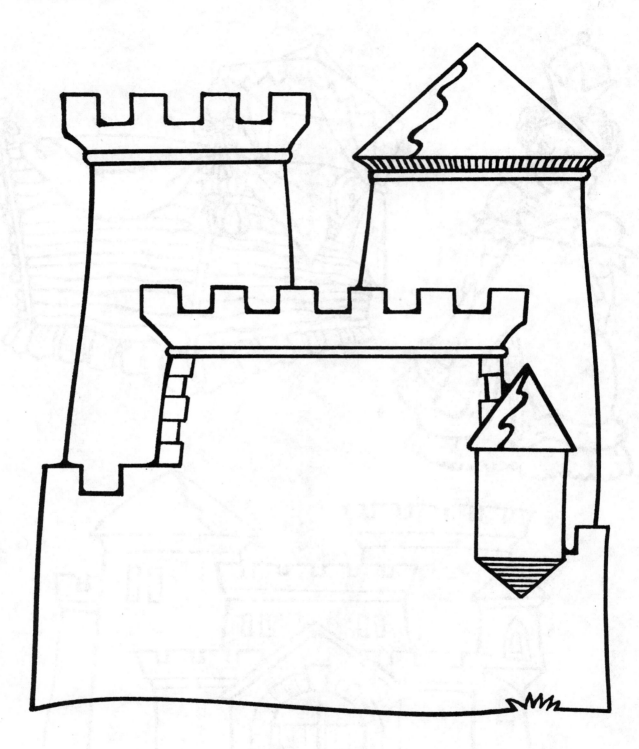

Name _____

The _____

and the _____

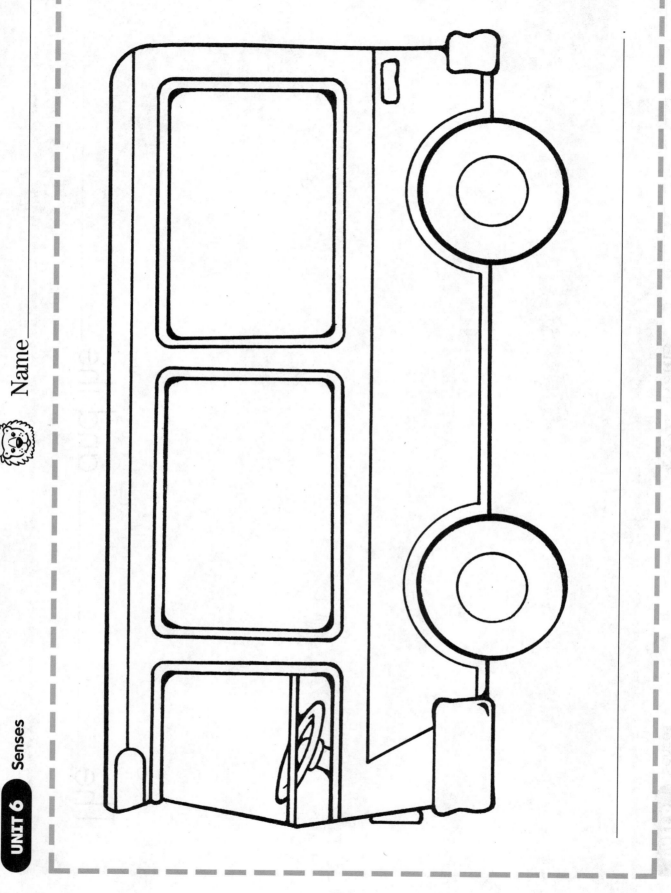

UNIT 6 Senses

UNIT 6 Senses

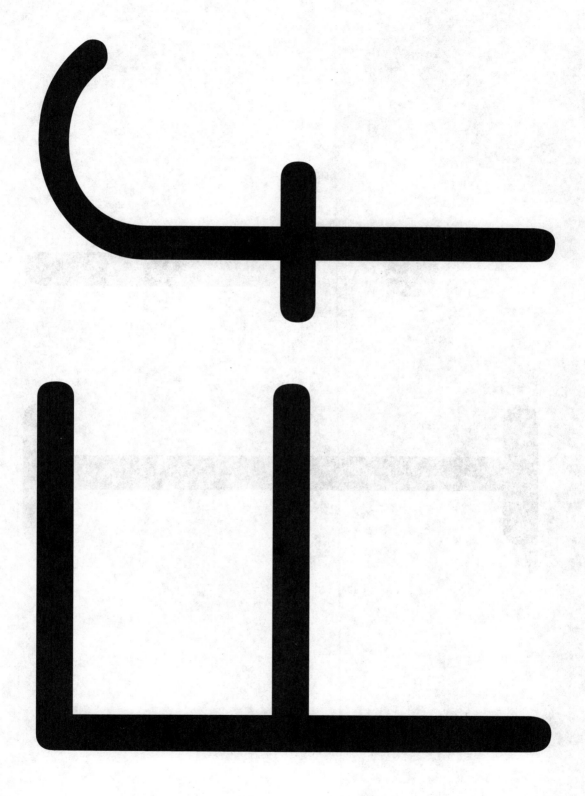

Teacher's Resource Book

Name

UNIT 6 Senses

The Animals on the Bus

Written and Drawn by _____

Name_____

A baby cow is a _____.

A baby duck is a _____.

A baby goat is a _____.

A baby chicken is a _____.

101

There are _____ in
the barn.

UNIT 7 At the Farm

Lesson 9

103

My biggest animal would

be a _____.

My smallest animal would be a _____.

I would grow _____.

If I Had a Farm . . .

Written and Drawn by

_____

Name_____

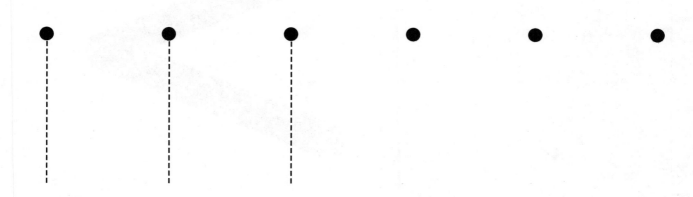

111

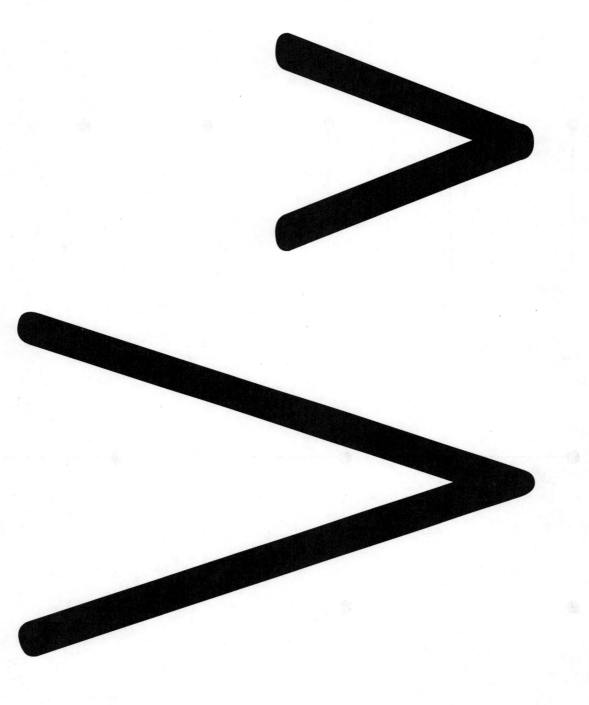

Name _____

In _____, _____ likes to _____.

113

Name_____

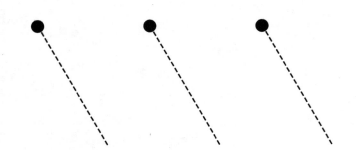

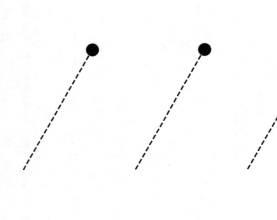

Name_____

Copyright © SRA/McGraw-Hill. Permission is granted to reproduce this page for classroom use.

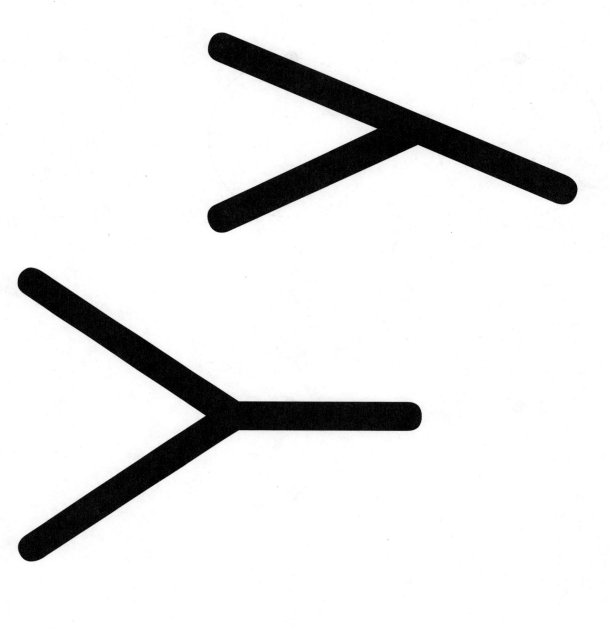

Teacher's Resource Book

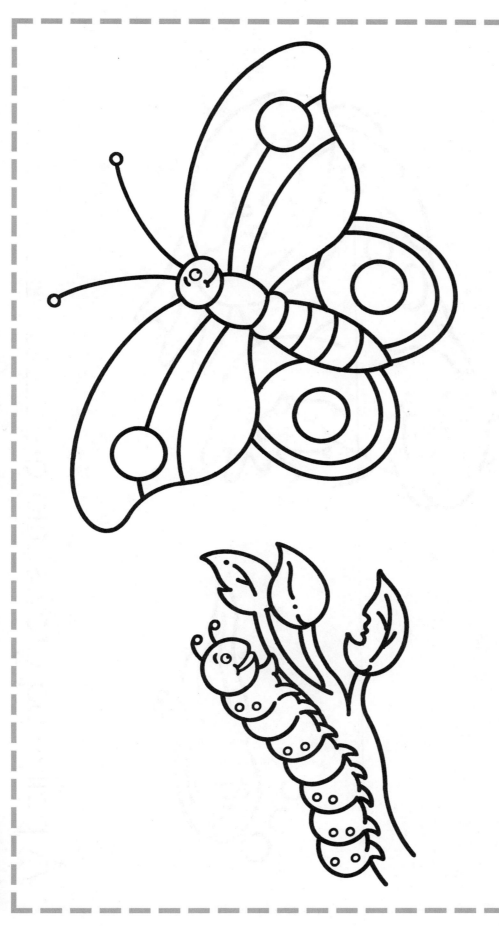

A caterpillar changes into a _____.

Name _____

A pollywog grows into a _____ .

Name_____

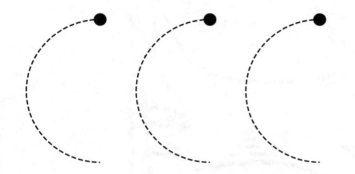

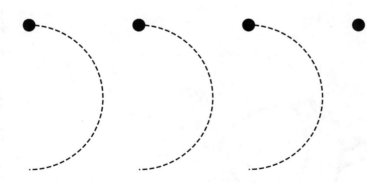

An acorn grows to be an _____ .

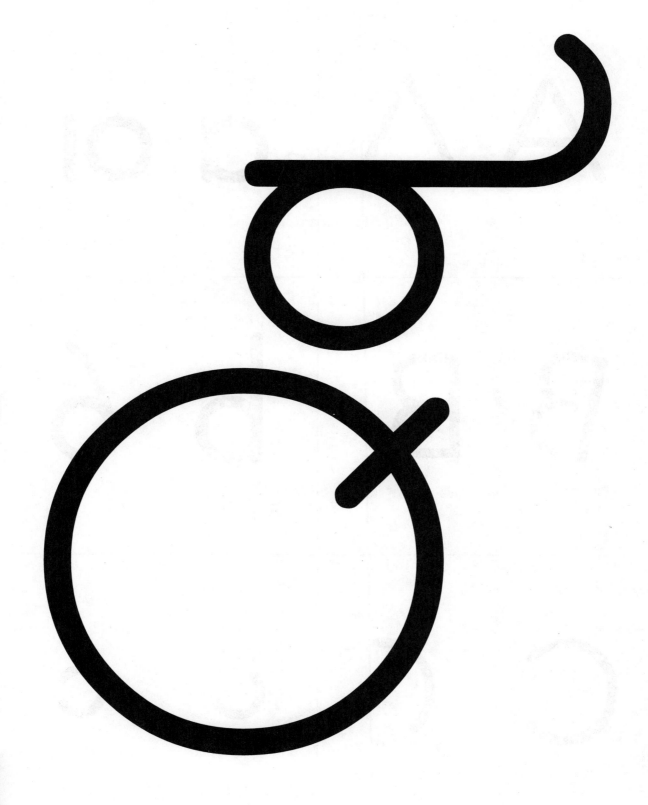

Name_____

A A   a o i

B B   b 6

C C   c c

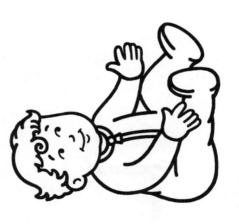

A baby grows into a _____ .

Name_____

D D D d d

E E e e

F Γ ſ f

G G G g q

H H h h

I I i i

Name

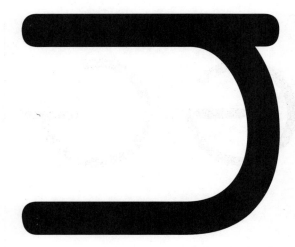

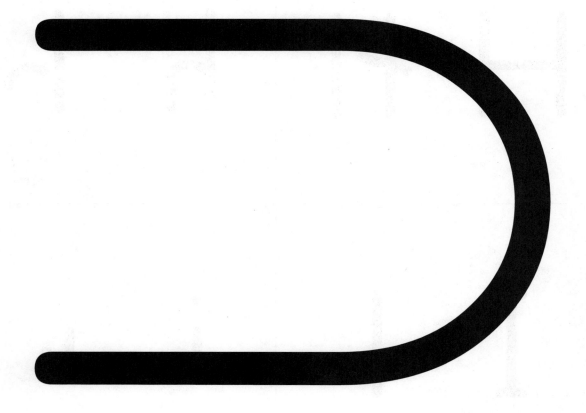

127

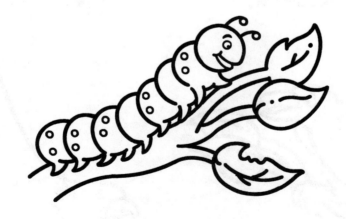

J J j j

K K k k

L L I \

Name_____

M M M m m

N N N ɦ n

O O o c

Name_____

P P P | P | ° P

∅ Q Q q q q

R R R ⌐ r ⌐ r

Name_____

S S S   s s

T T T   + +

U U U   u u

Name_____

V V v v

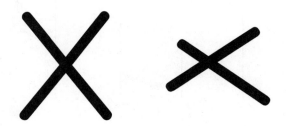

X X x x

Come to Our Final
Unit Celebration!

To: _____

Date: _____

Time: _____

Place: _____

From: _____

Y Y Y Y

1 Z z z

This year,

learned

136

Name _____

F Γ ∧ ∧

D D J J

M M ∧ Я R

Name_____

B B E E

N N G G

C C K K

138

Name_____

H H P P

S S Z Z

O O W W